minimalisms

Editorial Gustavo Gili, SA

08029 Barcelona   Rosselló, 87-89. Tel. 93 322 81 61

minimalisms

Anatxu Zabalbeascoa ▪ Javier Rodríguez Marcos

GG®

Cover design: Toni Cabré/Editorial Gustavo Gili, SA
Translation: Paul Hammond

© Editorial Gustavo Gili, SA, Barcelona, 2000

Printed in Spain
ISBN: 84-252-1809-8
Image Digitalization: Scan Gou
Depósito legal: B. 45.993-1999
Printing: Ingoprint, SA, Barcelona

contents

minimalisms
a sign of
the times?

As the philosophers are every now and then wont to recall, a specter is forever haunting the world. Some specters are born and disappear with the speed of this season's fashion. Others, though, haunt history and deck themselves out with various prefixes —pre, post, neo, trans— so as to go on breathing the air of the times. They arrive to stay or they come and go throughout a civilization, an era or a century, on which they leave an indelible mark. Such is the case, it would seem, with classicism, the baroque or modernism.

In a century like the twentieth, born in great haste, the phantoms glide over the decades, arguing among themselves, the word calming their nerves: *arte povera*, Pop, the new era, structuralism, high-tech, deconstruction... Each term has a precise content until it breaks the bounds of its own discipline and starts cutting across the landscape of the culture. As with so many others, this could well be the case with minimalism.

And so, thirty years or more after the birth of sculptural minimalism in the United States, we've moved the world over from minimalism to the minimal, whether we're talking music, literature, dance, design or architecture. What was once austere, plain or sober is now minimalist; or *minimal*, to use the popular English term.

To arrive at the maximum of expressivity using the minimum of expression has become the goal of creative people in every walk of life. "That plainness has such impact," says the Swiss architect Peter Zumthor, "bespeaks the excess of noise that has invaded the landscapes around us." In effect, in an era dripping with images, forms and sounds, to reduce, purge or filter ends up being the most eloquent gesture. When absence can be the most emphatic form of presence,

Donald Judd, *Untitled*, 1970. Brass and fluorescent plexiglass

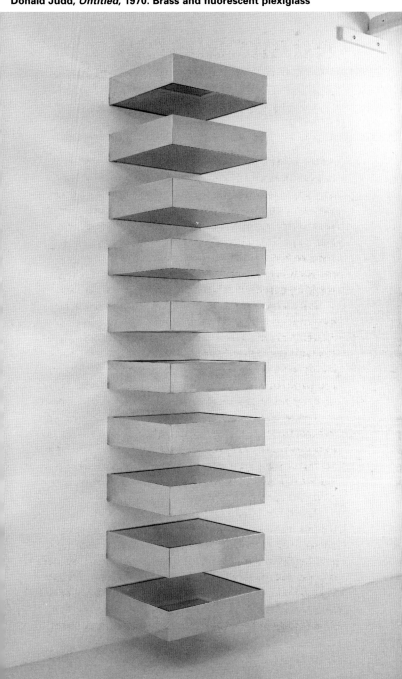

Wiel Arets, Police Station, Boxtel, Holland, 1997

stopping doing something manages to become a positive gesture. On occasions this doesn't even mean subtracting, but rather not adding. "If my work is reductionist it's because it doesn't contain the things people think it ought to contain," said Donald Judd, a man for whom, what's more, minimalism is less a system than a basic attitude, a way of perceiving the world.

On the other hand, just as any movement produces its own descendents, it could also be said to create, although this may seem paradoxical, its own precedents. From this viewpoint, one of the most rigorous minimalists of the century must have been an architect whose death all but coincides with minimalism's birth: Mies van der Rohe. While it's true that the theories of the Modern Movement embraced geometric essentiality and the absence of ornament, it's also true that the austere formal radicality and use of materials of current architects like Tadao Ando, John Pawson, Wiel Arets, Dominique Perrault or Zumthor himself have driven an even greater wedge between Mies and the functionalism of those who were his contemporaries, and have marked him out as an undoubted precursor of part of today's architecture.

For the German architect, as for many of the so-called minimalists, the plainness of a building is a choice rather than a limitation, a mixture of necessity and virtue. Commenting in 1953 on his chapel for ITT in Chicago, Mies van der Rohe wrote: "I opt for an intensive, rather than extensive, form (…) All too often we think about architecture in terms of spectacularness. There's nothing spectacular in the chapel; it aims to be plain; and in fact it is plain. Yet despite its plainness it isn't ordinary, but noble, and its truly monumental grandeur lies in its small size. I wouldn't have constructed the chapel any other way, even if I'd had a million bucks."

Then again, if minimalism occasionally implies a conscious step backwards, no work would illustrate that better than the Seagram Building built by Mies in New York. The edifice imposes its presence on Park Avenue by drawing discreetly back from the line of the street and creating a plaza, rather than relying on the usual ziggurat construction of New York's skyscrapers.

Mies van der Rohe, IIT Chapel, Chicago, 1952

Mies van der Rohe, Seagram Office Building, New York, 1958

Dominique Perrault, Book Center, Marne-la-Vallée, France, 1995

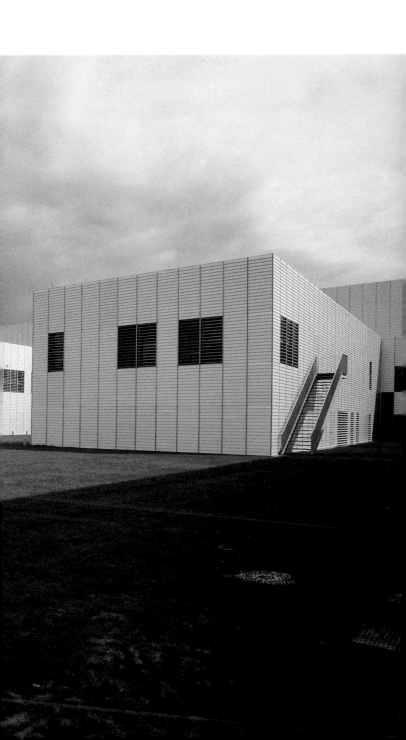

If we take minimalism to be a way of seeing as well as doing —or ceasing to do—, then it isn't strange that such a vision has broken through, as it has with history and geography. Thus, the oriental sobriety that seduced modern masters like Frank Lloyd Wright, Adolf Loos or Irving Gill has done just that for many contemporary architects, architects like Pawson who are interested in the moral aspects of austerity as well as the forms that this helps create. Alongside the idea of poverty as an inner luxury that subtends this philosophy, we would have, in passing, to set the connection Loos established between absence of ornament and intellectual strength. Similarly, Le Corbusier requested of the inhabitants of his houses that they have a new attitude and a "new spirit." As early as 1907 Mies van der Rohe, once again, had set into the stone wall of the Riehl House a word that summarized its spirit: *monastic*.

In a way, the combination of ascetic humility and aristocratic arrogance brought together in the minimalist attitude is but one of the many contradictions that such a basically transparent attitude is imbued with. Another, and no less significant, one would be the paradox that economy of means is not always translated into economy of cost, but rather the opposite. An absolute purity of forms and materials often requires fine raw materials or those provided by the latest technology, plus the input of craftsmen to guarantee a quality finish. In that sense, architectural minimalism —allowing for the fact that few architects would feel themselves represented by that label, or by any other— would be a sort of Modern Movement sublimated in the formal, one which undermines the criterion of economy of materials, time and energy defended since the beginning of the century.

The ultimate paradox, finally, would be in observing how the basically most neutral, and therefore anonymous and styleless, forms end up becoming the most striking and unmistakable. When all's said and done, there's nothing as recognizable as a galvanized-steel cube by Donald Judd or an immaculately white interior by John Pawson.

Be that as it may, the identification of plainness with minimalism, like any generalization, transcends its own

Erwin Heerich, Insel Hombroich Museum, Neuss, Germany, 1982-

Rafael Moneo, Kursaal, San Sebastian, 1999

contradictions and transcends both the arts and the artists who make it. Hence, an architect such as Rafael Moneo, so innately distinct from the real minimalists, has recourse to such a language in individual projects like the Kursaal in San Sebastián. The same could be said of Rem Koolhaas's house with two patios. On occasion, a building born of a mixing of styles incorporates the sobriety of minimalism. This is the case with Hans Hollein's Abteiberg Museum.

For better or worse, in recent years phrases like geometric purity, technical precision, structural essentiality, the repetition of elements and materials, abstraction and ornamental purification have been, and are, frequently summed up in —when not identified with— a single word whose immediate influence in everyday language has gone way beyond its actual definition: minimalism.

Time alone will tell whether this is nothing other than the latest eye-catching disguise that technology and craftsmanship offer to architectural modernism, the final move, beyond history, towards an eternal classicism, or a genuine sign and style of our times, destined to survive both the styles and the times themselves.

Hans Hollein, Municipal Museum Abteiberg, Mönchengladbach, Germany, 1982

an intransitive art

The fate of the labels subdividing the history of art has often been due less to the conviction of their defenders than to the persistence of their detractors. From this point of view, and as in so many movements contested in their day but uncontestable now, the minimal never existed. It never existed, at least for the artists who in a precise time and place, the United States in the 60s, were identified with the label. "The word minimalism," Donald Judd argued years later, "is a word I don't like. It wasn't a group, nor was it a movement... What was called the minimal group was all pie in the sky. We didn't even know each other."

If the controversy about who the minimalists were was a long one, the doubts about which name to give to what we now call minimalist art lasted somewhat less time. 'Primary structures', 'specific objects', 'ABC art', 'negative art', 'literalism' and 'nihilist art' were some of the words bandied about in criticisms of the new art's first exhibitions. Finally, in January 1965 an article by Richard Wollheim appeared, the title of which would be a hit in all languages: 'Minimal Art'. Oddly enough, in that text Duchamp, Mallarmé and Rauschenberg were discussed, but not the artists who would later be associated with the tendency Wollheim was unwittingly baptizing: Carl Andre, Donald Judd, Dan Flavin, Sol Le Witt and Robert Morris, in the main.

The problem of the name being resolved, what might the common denominator be linking those five artists? Put another way, and taking on board the necessarily reductive nature of such a question, what are the general characteristics of minimalism? A first response would be to sum these up as abstraction, elementary geometry, austerity and

Donald Judd, *Untitled*, 1972. Copper, enamel and aluminum

Carl Andre, *144 Magnesium Square*, 1969. Magnesium

Dan Flavin, *Ursula's One and Two Picture 1/3,* 1964. Ultraviolet fluorescent light

monochromatism. Taking this viewpoint further, we might add repetition. A minimalist work, then, would be a simple three-dimensional composition with regular, rectilinear geometrical forms, lacking in compositional effects and ornamentation.

In any event, the more usual definitions of minimalism have focused on the negative aspect of the image; that is, have relied on affirming what it isn't in order to approximate to what it is. To begin with, this tendency transcends artistic genres as these are traditionally considered, since it isn't, in the strict sense, either painting or sculpture. It isn't painting because the works have volume and renounce the illusionism that working on a two-dimensional surface implies; it isn't sculpture because, despite their volume and their three-dimensional nature, the works lack certain qualities, lack composition. "The ordering isn't rationalist or essential, just simple ordering, such as continuity, one thing behind another," Donald Judd stated in 1964 in reference to his own work and that of Frank Stella. Along the same non-pictorial and non-sculptural lines, Sol Le Witt spoke of structures and Dan Flavin of schemes. Judd himself referred to his works as specific objects, works which are not the sign of anything and have no other referent than themselves, hence their specificity. "Totally free art does not have its outcome in a painting or a sculpture, but in a pure object," André Malraux wrote in terms that would have pleased Judd if they hadn't been formulated in Europe, given that avoiding European tradition as much as possible was a basic premise for the more radical minimalists.

Turning the sentence around which claims that what has a history cannot have a definition, we might say that if artistic minimalism presents a thousand problems as to definition, it undoubtedly has a history. And a geography.

As chance would have it, at the height of the convulsive 60s equally strong winds were blowing in the Old and the New World. The discrediting of the expressive capacity of language in twentieth-century philosophy had taken two very different roads. One led to silence, which in artistic terms involved the so-called closure of representation. More than a critique aimed at the idea of truth, this was, if this isn't the same thing, aimed at its possibilities of expression. More than at reality, at its appearance. The other road led to the things themselves, to use an often invoked formula of Husserl's. This was the tack taken by the writers of the *nouveau roman*. For them the world is neither absurd nor full of meaning, it simply is. Instead of the traditional universe of signifieds —psychological, social, metaphysical, emotional or functional— the question was to build a more solid, more immediate world, neither personal or subjective, neither tragic or narrative. This was to mean, finally, positing gestures and objects as things in their own right.

The second route is oriented, then, towards pure referentiality, towards a sort of ideal pragmatism in which saying and wishing to say coincide. This is the road of the purest realism, of presentation as opposed to representation, the road that leads to the specificity of objects. The works born of this spirit appeal more to description than to interpretation, since they respond to strictly formal problems.

Working along these lines, the minimalists tried to create new relationships of volume, color and scale. Equally, they tried to rethink the relationship between art as a (specific) object and between the object and man the artist. Such was the new approach produced in the United States in the 60s.

The art scene was dominated by Abstract Expressionism at the time. The Abstract Expressionists posited a direct link between the artist's inner psychology and painting's illusionist interior. Art was, then, converted into a metaphor of the human emotions. "Painting, which is an act, is inseparable from the artist's biography (…) Art devolves to painting via psychology," Harold Rosenberg wrote apropos of action painting. In a sense, one had gone down a rung on the ladder the avant-gardes had used to arrive at the complete autonomy of the art object. The reaction against Abstract Expressionism was not only to make up for those lost rungs, but begin to ascend them two by two. This, following in the footsteps of Marcel Duchamp, would be the attitude that soon gave rise to Pop Art and, a little later on, to conceptual art. It would also be, rejecting blazed trails *per se* and walking on empty air, the minimalists' attitude.

Poles apart from all psychologism, a total rejection resulted of an ideal inner space existing prior to its own

formal creation. That rejection was materialized in works
that negated the uniqueness, privacy and inaccessibility
of experience. The work could be immediately grasped in
its entirety. All there was to see in objects was their actual
presence. Anybody could understand them at first sight.
According to that viewpoint, the meaning of a work proceeded
more from a public space than from a private, internal and
inaccessible one. Whence Pop Art's interest in mass culture
and the universal aspirations of neutral minimalist geometry,
the radical abstraction of which tries to eliminate all presence
of the human body in its works and hinder the projection
of any psychological bias in them. "No illusions, no illusions,"
Donald Judd said.

The notions of geometric abstraction, austerity and
monochromatism present in many artistic tendencies was
now consolidated in a search for a maximum expressivity
—without expressionisms— arrived at with the minimum
of means. In this way the specificity of minimalist objects,
aside from being abstract and austere, was engendered,
in the first place, by the industrial and literal use they made
of certain materials. Secondly, spanning the forms and
attitudes, by being shown without a frame or pedestal,
by their concentration on surface as opposed to interior,
their decentering and dehumanization and by their distance
from any tradition, however avant-garde.

The use of industrial materials —bricks, steel, aluminum,
plastic, copper, fluorescent light, mirrors and sheets of glass—
and the industrial production of the works themselves led to
a perfect abstraction of finish and erased all signs of the
artist's intervention. Here, the galvanized, lacquered or
enamel-painted surface triumphs over patina and oil paint.
The choice of a material is the taking of a position. In this
way the traditional bonding of the sculptor with his materials
is overcome and the hierarchical relationships of a
compositional layout of elements avoided, since their
'assembly-line production' means that each of the objects
will have the same size and form.

In the article that helped give minimalism its name,
Richard Wollheim evokes the ancient relationship between
art and manual effort via a question which, in his opinion,

the readymades of Duchamp or the monochrome canvases of Ad Reinhart had rendered obsolete: what is the meaning of the word 'work' in the phrase 'work of art'?

"Not getting my hands dirty is crucial as far as I'm concerned," Dan Flavin said. "I insist on art as a way of thinking." The artist's way of working approximates, then, to that of the architect, who plans but never personally executes his designs. On the other hand, the defence of art as idea would come close, for some, to the terrain of conceptual art, an area in which Sol Le Witt's contribution was crucial.

As well as being produced industrially, the materials in minimalist works are used literally, they aren't disguised or manipulated in order to seem like something else or to seem invisible. This, then, is to break with the kind of sculpture that, for instance, represents human flesh by using marble, passing from the literal to the metaphorical and converting one material into the sign of another. Eschewing all illusionism, objects are interesting for their material, form, color and volume, taken for what they are, not for what they might represent. "My painting," Frank Stella argued, "is based on the fact that only what can be seen is there. It's really an object (...) What you see is what you see."

This entailed, as we saw, passing from representation to presentation, from the sphere of appearances to the sphere of realities. In objects without a narrative or representational ambition —either figurative or abstract— the spectator can grasp the idea, form and qualities of a work in an instant. The meaning and potential beauty of these primary structures resided in classical formal aspects: order, proportion, measure or rhythm.

Some critics have attempted to trace the genealogy of minimalism from the essential geometric abstraction of Malevich's white-on-white picture. Others have singled out Jorge Oteiza's work in the 50s as a kind of sculptural proto-minimalism. Meanwhile, at a certain moment Robert Morris and Dan Flavin, who dedicated one of his light installations to Tatlin, took the Russian Constructivists to be the initiators of the autonomous tradition in modern sculpture. For his part, Carl Andre paid a lot of attention to the work of

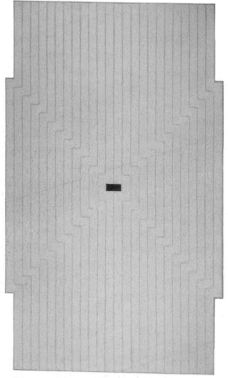

**Frank Stella, *Six Mile Bottom*, 1960.
Metallic paint on canvas**

Carl Andre, *Lever 1966*. Firebricks

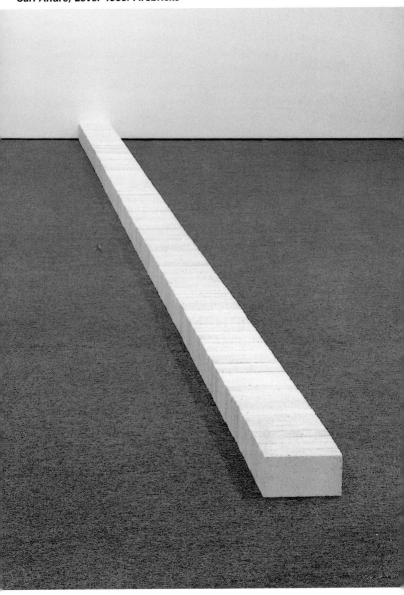

Brancusi, whose 'Endless Column' is crucial to the design of his own work, 'Lever'.

It was Donald Judd, however, who most radically established the difference between the American minimalists and their possible European forebears. In the essentialism of the latter there persisted an element of the expressionist ambition, which Judd set out to eliminate: composition. The artist sought to dispense with compositions and compensations, and thereby to avoid the anthropomorphism that, in his opinion, any interrelating of the parts brings with it, even in the works of Mondrian, Kandinsky and Malevich. When describing the different elements used in some of his works Judd was crystal clear: one thing behind another. "A simple form, let's say a box," he said, "has, in effect, an order, but it isn't so ordered that that is its main quality. The more parts a thing has the more important the order is, until this finally becomes the most important thing of all. My works are symmetrical because I wanted to rid myself of any compositional effect, and the most obvious way of doing this is symmetry (...) Such effects tend to bring with them all the structures, values and emotions of the European tradition."

A few years earlier, in 1958, Mies van der Rohe, a European exiled in the United States whose work has been frequently linked to that of the minimalists, also made reference to symmetry. He did so while commenting on the Crown Hall and the Mannheim Theater on the ITT campus in Chicago, and he spoke of it as an effect more than a cause: "Why can't they be symmetrical? In the majority of the buildings on this campus it's perfectly natural that there are flights of steps on both sides and that the auditorium and lobby are in the middle. Hence it's natural that the buildings turn out symmetrical."

It didn't take long for contradictory discourses, situated somewhere between tradition and wiping the slate clean, to appear around the theme of minimalism. They all agreed, however, on one thing: that its emergence substantially altered the look of art, how it's made and what it's made of. The consensus ended there, because agreement didn't seem possible in respect of something that has no respect for what it means.

Robert Morris, *Untitled,* **1965-1971. Mirror plate glass and wood**

Leonardo da Vinci, A Puzzle Construction, 1490

Sol Le Witt, *Five Modular Structures,* **1972**

For some, the work of certain minimalists is so directly related to European rationalist philosophy as to constitute the true likeness of such thinking. Donald Kuspit speaks of the work of Sol Le Witt in these terms: "On occasions, the most elaborate of these constructions appear to be translations of philosophical systems to a purely formal language. If anyone can perceive the structural beauty of Descartes or Kant's work, and recreate this as an exclusively visual metaphor, that person is surely Sol Le Witt."

Other critics, meanwhile, are opposed to an idealist reading of minimalist geometry. If for them regularity and repetition are variants of a rational order, this does not involve pure reason but rather its opposite, the outpourings of a chaotic mind. The work is exactly the opposite of the semblance of thought, understanding this as the classical expression of logic. Judged this way, minimalist works would be closer to one of Beckett's obsessive characters than to Kant or Descartes. A supposed constructivist paternity would be no more than a self-serving search for legitimacy. "It doesn't matter," writes Rosalind Krauss contra the legitimators, "that Gabo's celluloids might be the sign of lucidity and intellect, that Judd's day-glo-tinted plastics might speak the hippest Californian dialect. It doesn't matter that Constructivist forms might have been conceived as a visual demonstration of the coherence and immutable logic of universal geometries, and that their seemingly minimalist counterparts were explicitly contingent, that they might denote a universe whose unity was not due to the Understanding, but to mere wires, or to glue, or the casual effect of gravity."

While minimalist works reject any historicist, metaphorical or impressionistic reading —"The inner man does not exist," Merleau-Ponty would say—, their effect is necessarily registered in one's perception, not in what the things mean, that they mean no more than that of being things, but in how they are perceived. Their form and positioning encourages reflection on the relative nature of perspective and the circumstances of the place in which they are found, including the architecture.

Michael Benedikt underlined the relationship between minimalist object and architectural space in an early review of the pieces exhibited by Morris and Judd in New York's Dwan Gallery in 1967. "Morris' sculpture," Benedikt writes, "was a white block ten feet wide that drew the attention in a particular way to the limits of the gallery, especially towards the walls, to which they had a great similarity. Although grayish, the line of six boxes of galvanized iron also seemed to sculpt the space outside, drawing the eye more to the space around them than to their own." Sculpture and architecture were beginning to eradicate the barriers between them.

Is it architecture or is it still sculpture?

"Sculpture is what you bang into when you step back to see a painting." It could be said that the history of twentieth-century art is a process that has ended up denying the truth of this quip of Barnett Newman's. Sculpture is no longer, to use Rosalind Krauss' phrase, "what was on or in front of a building yet wasn't the building, or what was in the landscape yet wasn't the landscape."

It's enough to glance at the evolution of contemporary sculpture to see how its scope has gone on expanding and modifying its relationship to painting, buildings or the landscape. While minimalism is a good example of an interaction with the pictorial, and Land Art operates directly on the natural setting, other, varying aspects contribute to the sculpture's orientation towards domains hitherto claimed by architecture.

In the first place, we have to consider the tendency of modern sculpture to distance itself from figuration and from the logic of the monument. With this distancing, sculpture leans towards the representation of its own materials and towards the fetishization of the base, the appropriation of the plinth, something Brancusi was the precursor of. The new preoccupation with creating abstract forms in space exactly coincides with a traditional investigation of architecture.

Secondly, sculptors begin to work with the new materials —concrete, steel, glass— and building techniques architecture had gradually taken over from industry.

Lastly, the architecture of the Modern Movement itself had evolved via a purification that superseded traditional historical styles. Bypassing caryatids and decorative frills, the paths of architecture and sculpture were both moving side by side in the direction of abstraction. Although use of the word minimalism has extended from the visual arts to a part of today's architecture, the sobriety of the Modern Movement in architecture has had more influence on sculpture than the other way round, at least in purely chronological terms.

In 1957 a work was designed in Mexico City that became a landmark for certain minimalists: the sculptor and architect Mathias Goeritz's set of 'Satellite City Towers' for a plaza designed by Mario Pani and Luis Barragán. The work consists of a group of monumental reinforced-concrete elements, five prismatic volumes looking like functionless buildings. Although Goeritz argued for the validity of a set of values far distant from the interests of the American minimalists —"we need faith, we need God, we need cathedrals and pyramids, we need better and more meaningful art," he said— his work followed the same path towards total abstraction.

The use of basic geometry, industrial techniques, pure surfaces and the search for simple, immediately comprehensible images were all premises of minimalist sculpture which can be said to constitute, for architecture, the culmination of the premises of modernism.

On the other hand, some minimalist pieces depend conceptually and physically on architecture. As simple rectilinear shapes, they repeat the forms of architecture, their positioning is parallel to the planes making up the building; the floor, ceiling and walls. They turn the architecture into an active support instead of a passive container. In the 60s the new sculpture moved from creating objects or structures located in space to planning pieces that defined a space.

In these circumstances the interest of architects in sculptors, and vice-versa, has nothing strange about it. Aside from the fact that Tony Smith, a precursor of minimalism, worked as a draughtsman for Frank Lloyd Wright, or that Sol Le Witt was a draughtsman in the I. M. Pei studio for a while, a *Zeitgeist* exists that's based on essentiality. It suffices to note the forthright presence of Pei's Everson Museum in Syracuse (1962), or the purity of color of Richard Meier's Museum für Kunsthandwerk (1985).

Luis Barragán, Mathias Goeritz, *Torres de la Ciudad Satélite,*
Mexico D.F., 1957

The same family atmosphere could be said to exist between Robert Morris' monoliths and certain of Simon Ungers' installations. Or between Isozaki's Gunma City Museum, the 'conceptual axonometry' of Tadao Ando's Koshino house and the structures of Sol Le Witt. Or, lastly, between the latter's drawings and Pei's grid for the Louvre pyramid. In fact, both sides are interested in a conceptualization of space as materialized in the constructed work.

In Le Witt's work architectonic space takes on a relevance that extends beyond the status of mere backdrop, something that Dan Flavin's work takes to an extreme. For Flavin, although architecture works with space, one's perception of this space can be altered just as much by light as by some more solid material. This dialectic between space and light can also be observed in the light-filled installations of James Turrell and in Steven Holl's design for the Shaw & Company Offices.

Likewise, Carl Andre's work tries to slowly do away with volume, and even its presence in space, in order to become one with it. Components protruding no more than a few millimeters from the floor they sit on respond to a moment at the beginning of the 70s when Andre considered that his first work was too sculptural, too structural, even: it could be said that a similar spirit informs both an installation like 'Equivalent I-VIII' from 1966 and Mies van der Rohe's ITT plan from 1941. At a certain moment Andre wanted his works to be more like road surfaces than like buildings, as he put it.

Prior to that radical shift towards the absolute minimum —or towards the conceptual—, it is a concern for the structural that furthers direct use of materials in Andre or an interest in removing the skin and revealing the structure in Le Witt. Frank Stella, meanwhile, tries to establish total continuity between the structural and the superficial. For him, the logic of compositional structure is inseparable from the logic of the sign, which is why the paint on the canvas simply follows the shape of the stretcher. In Donald Judd truth to materials is aimed, in the opposite way to those that work using light, at eliminating illusory effects of any kind, so that the represented space is at one with real space. Judd

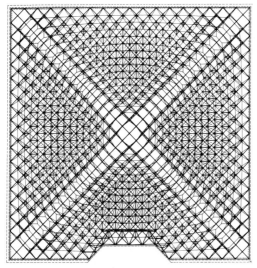

I. M. Pei, Louvre Pyramid, plan, Paris, 1989

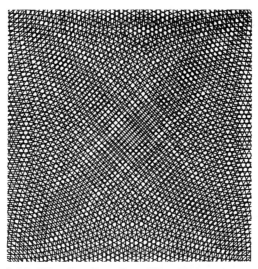

Sol Le Witt, *Arcs From Four Sides*, 1971

Snøhetta, Fishing Museum, Karmøy, Norway, 1998

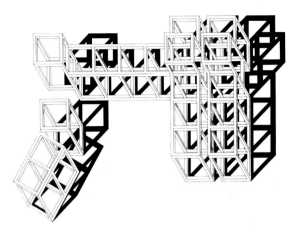

**Arata Isozaki, Museum of Modern Art,
Gunma, Japan, 1974**

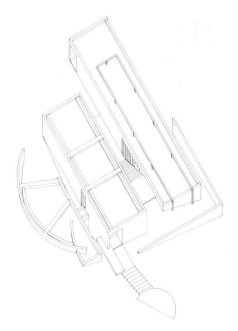

**Tadao Ando, Koshino House, axonometric,
Hyogo, Japan, 1981**

Robert Morris, *Two Columns,* **1973. Painted aluminum**

Simon Ungers, *9 x 9 x 9,* **1997**

Simon Ungers, *Cantilever,* **1994**

James Turrell, *Heavy Water***, 1991**

Carl Andre, *Equivalent I-VIII,* **1996. Sand-lime bricks**

Mies van der Rohe, IIT Campus, photomontage of master plan,
Chicago, 1941

elaborates and reduces his objects until their form coincides with their constituent elements.

In this he coincides with Mies van der Rohe's defence of a building having most purity while it is still being erected and its structure can be seen, since it's this that gives it its form.

It's within this context that we must situate the early interest the minimalist sculptors displayed in an unprecedented architectonic typology, the main contribution of the Modern Movement, converted into an international style, to the urban landscape: the skyscraper. The pure prisms Mies built on 860 and 880 Lake Shore Drive in Chicago (1951) and, above all, the Seagram in New York (1958) attain maximum presence of the minimum through the transparency of their surfaces, the geometrically pure form of their outlines and their use of industrial materials.

One could add to this their emphatic presence in the city fabric, due to their scale and volume, something which suggests a system of perception similar to that of certain of Robert Morris' works, which play with the relationship between objective knowledge and subjective experience. It suffices to think of the possibility or impossibility, depending on the perspective, of managing to take in a skyscraper from the street, something which, among other things, led Mies to create a plaza in front of the Seagram.

For some, the problem of the new skyscrapers is reduced to their presence in the city grid, an external presence that takes its cue from two defining elements: their outline and their facade. On the face of it, the use of simple geometry and a uniformity of color and texture that, for example, the curtain wall gives to the facade links these skyscrapers to sculptural minimalism's emphatic prisms.

Converted into an open language rather than a closed style, minimalism offered a set of devices and forms to many artists —Bruce Nauman, Damien Hirst, Eva Hesse, Félix González Torres, James Turrell, Dan Graham or Rodney Graham— who used, and use, minimalist forms with considerable irony, or at least with certain concerns that go way beyond pure objectuality.

An artist like Dan Graham tries to take a position somewhere in between. For him both cold, conceptual

Mies van der Rohe, 860-880 North Lake Shore Drive Apartment Buildings, Chicago, 1951

Dan Graham, *Double exposure*, 1996

abstraction and social realism end up being rhetorical, which is why he tries to provide the former with a function and the latter with an aesthetic form. Graham, who was the gallery owner behind Sol Le Witt's first exhibition in 1964, believes in the dialectical nature of all cultural discourse, which should in his opinion reveal the artificiality of ideological representations. For him artistic neutrality can be translated into political neutrality, something that in the United States is the equivalent of conservatism. For Dan Graham art and architecture are social —political and economic— signs. And so he criticizes the aseptic purism of both the minimalists and certain modern architects who take themselves to be beyond current circumstances, context and ideology. Thus the artist endows apparently minimalist pieces with an interior and a function. As well as being livable in, a number of his constructions reflect kaleidoscopic images of nature, the spectator and its own structure by day. By night the interior is visible, like some big International-Style office building.

In a sense we could say that the post-minimalist sculptors attempted to go beyond self-sufficient, aseptic formalism, in much the same way that a number of end-of-the-century architects, the so-called minimalists, who remain faithful to the modern inheritance of an austere tradition, try to adapt their achievements to the times without falling into the kind of fundamentalism or disdain for context that has sometimes seen the best of intentions turn into the worst of results.

Eva Hesse, *Accession II*, 1969. Galvanized steel and rubber tubing

Damien Hirst, *The Physical Impossibility of Death in the Mind of Someone Living,* **1991. Tiger shark, glass, steel, formaldehyde solution**

the zero degree of architecture

It could almost certainly be argued that the sober forms that have had so much success in recent times do not proceed from 60s minimalist sculpture, but from the architecture of the Modern Movement. It is more likely that while the word was coined in the 60s, the concept it designates was crystalizing slowly in a tendency towards abstraction present in all the arts at the beginning of the twentieth century, from painting and sculpture to architecture, taking in theater, music and design, and from Russian Constructivism to the Bauhaus, not to mention Dutch Neo-Plasticism.

Notwithstanding the fact that the more radical American minimalists sought, as we saw, to have done with European tradition, the constructions we now call minimalist have their antecedents not so much in the cubes of Donald Judd, Robert Morris or Sol Le Witt but in the designs of Adolf Loos, Le Corbusier and Mies van der Rohe.

To be sure, many of the procedures utilized by the minimalists had been proposed and put into practice in architecture by the Modern Movement. All we need to do is think of architecture's abstraction, economy of language and means, its industrial production techniques, literal use of materials and absence of ornament.

If minimalist works tried to eliminate any allusion alien to their own objectuality, architecture, too, and prior to any other art perhaps, sought to eliminate any reference and free itself of the straitjacket of historical styles that had hitherto determined all form, composition and materials according to a fixed repertoire. Oddly enough, art and architecture would pursue the same objectives along roads that were formally parallel but philosophically different, opposed even. Sculpture freed itself of the yoke of anthropomorphism, in the form of statues and monuments, by recourse to an absolute abstraction oblivious to any symbol and function beyond that of pure form. For its part, architecture took the road of functionalism as its way out: form would be strictly determined by function, with no stylistic or figurative concessions.

Paradoxically, the new architectural credo of the International Style imposed its hegemony right up until the early days of sculptural minimalism, when, having become a form of scholasticism applied massively and indiscriminately throughout the world, and one oblivious to the cultural and climactic factors that mean Rio de Janeiro and Helsinki are two very different cities, it began to fall apart. Despite this, and over and above the degeneration resulting from the inflexible application of its teachings, the masters of the Modern Movement instigated a move towards simplicity that still persists today.

At the time of *L'Esprit Nouveau*, during the 20s, Le Corbusier argued for the transcending of Cubism because in his opinion the times called for a spirit of exactitude unattainable via that language, although he applauded it for having reduced form to its geometrical elements. As against Cubism, the Swiss architect launched an even more radical aesthetic: Purism.

The purist idea in architecture, though, wasn't always related to the structural or functional purity that would ultimately impose itself. Peter Collins, an historian of the ideals of modern architecture, observes that a certain notion of purity would have a strong aesthetic, not to say aestheticist, component that goes beyond the strict functional necessity defended by Le Corbusier himself, or the exaltation of structure as a source of form defended by Mies. As it was, this purity called for total dissimulation of a building's structure. The surface areas were left completely smooth because of the interest 'pure'

Le Corbusier, La Roche-Jeanneret House, Paris, 1923

surfaces held, and when there were structural elements these were uniformly plastered over. "Interiors were reduced to white walls with one or two abstract paintings hung on them," Collins writes, "and the entire architecture was given the appearance of an operating theater."

Of course, the image of an operating theater was evoked in the preface to Le Corbusier's *Vers une architecture*, with a quotation taken from a magazine: "Given their absolute suitedness, the operating theaters of modern hospitals are the world's most perfect rooms." Perhaps this obsession with apparent purity is the same one that, thanks to the latest technical means, has become part and parcel of the structural purity in the work of today's minimal architects.

There always were voices raised against such an obsessive preoccupation, voices like that of the Austrian writer Robert Musil, scandalized by the radicalism of certain schemes. "Modern man," the author of *The Man Without Qualities* wrote apropos of new housing, "is born in a hospital and dies in a hospital. Must he also live in a hospital? This is precisely what the avant-garde architect requires of him."

For Musil the avant-garde architect might well have been his compatriot Adolf Loos. When in 1925 Le Corbusier decrees in his essay 'The Decorative Art of Today' that modern decoration isn't decorative he in fact cites Loos as a precursor.

In 1898 Loos had published 'The City of Potemkin', attacking the tendency led by John Ruskin, who considered that architecture was the highest form of pure ornament, and attacking earlier Viennese trends in building. In this article Loos criticized the excess of false ornament, not so much decoration in itself as the imitation, in concrete, of details from Renaissance and baroque palaces. In his view such an attitude entailed giving up the search for a new language based on the new materials that had come on the scene after the Industrial Revolution.

A few years later, in 1908, Loos would give further point to his argument in 'Ornament and Offence'. For the architect the evolution of culture is proportional to the disappearance

Adolf Loos, Steiner House, Vienna, 1910

of ornament in utilitarian objects, and the greatness of the modern era lies in the fact that it is incapable of offering a new kind of ornamentation.

Loos, for all that, speaks from a position of plain arrogance: "I preach to the aristocrats," he says. For him the absence of ornament is a sign of intellectual strength and civilization. On top of that, he introduces notions that, a far cry from a purely formal assessment, lead him to expound on the superiority of European culture over, for example, African culture, ever in thrall to body painting and tattooing. That said, 'Ornament and Offence' contains pertinent reflections on the economy of time and means that the absence of decoration brings with it. "The ornamentalist," writes Loos, "has to work twenty hours to reach the income of a modern worker who works eight. The lack of ornament leads to a diminution of work time and a raising of wages."

For Loos, furthermore, the ideal thing is that an object's form is maintained intact for as long as the object exists. Sobriety, then, would resist fluctuations in fashion and changes of taste much better.

Notwithstanding this, and despite the importance of Loos and Le Corbusier, it is surely Mies van der Rohe who took abstraction and essentiality to their extremes. He is also the architect whose influence has been greatest within the International Style. Yet he is also the one whose attention to details and materials places him closest to the preoccupations of today's minimalists.

Once again, though, despite the family feeling he shares with many of the attitudes of visual minimalism, Mies van der Rohe centers all his ideas about architecture on an invisible, transcendental sense that goes beyond pure form, however economical the latter may be. Be that as it may, such distantiation coexists with ideas that are of interest to both.

In 1928 Mies launches a declaration that will resound over the years: "Architecture is always the spatial expression of an intellectual decision." For the architect this affirmation brings an order into operation, an order founded on spiritual principles which establishes a rapport between fact and meaning, object and subject, and gives meaning to life.

If intellectual decision-making gives rise to an order, this order takes place in a precise undertaking, so simple and so aware of its goal that the minimum of elements arrive at the maximum of expressivity.

Order as such is a fundamental term from very early on in the Miesian vocabulary. In 1921, in the manifesto in the magazine *G*, which the architect published in Berlin together with Hans Richter and El Lissitzky, these words appear: "The basic objective of *G* is economy. Pure relation of power and material. Fundamental order. Regularity."

Although the magazine was born under the influence of Theo van Doesburg's Neo-Plasticism, it isn't difficult to detect the echoes of classicism and its various versions in the search for such a fundamental order. "In the eighteenth century," Joseph Maseck wrote, "the word 'order' was almost enough to provoke erotic excitement." Notwithstanding this, and despite the importance Schinkel's neo-classicism had for Mies, his work does not rely on quotation, it doesn't try to resuscitate an epoch, but rather its spirit. It posits a classicism that transcends the historic and seeks to attain classical purity due to the elimination of all secondary features.

In Mies van der Rohe's case, and with a complete clarity that will not be evident, later, in the American minimalist sculptors, an analogy is made between rational thought and built work. Simple regularity, abstraction and the purest of constructional rules are aimed at attaining the maximum possible dematerialization. In this way the process of abstraction sought to reduce the object and to reveal the essential form hidden within it. In that sense, simple geometry would be the highest symbol of that fundamental and objective idea.

Despite all the nuances, Mies never abandoned the idea of an interior essence that transcends the exterior form and gives an authentic sense to the work. In his opening speech as head of the ITT architecture department in Chicago in 1938 he said: "We seek an order that gives each object its place. And we seek to give to each object that which

Karl Friedrich Schinkel, Charlottenburg Pavilion, Berlin, 1825

corresponds to it in its essence. We seek to do all this in so perfect a way that the world of our creations begins to blossom from within."

The search for that essential core led him to often repeat two phrases, from Saint Augustine and Saint Thomas respectively, which give an idea of the Platonism of his ideas *vis-à-vis* the aesthetic revelation of truth: "Beauty is the radiance of truth" and "Truth is the identity between thought and thing." From this viewpoint, the beautiful is not a subjective creation, but a reality in itself.

Given the intimate relationship between the two quotes above, for Mies only the authentic can be beautiful. It could be said that, in taking the opposite path, the German architect reached the same goal as the minimalists in terms of the handling of materials: if authenticity alone guarantees beauty, literal use of materials and attention to detail in the finishes has to be total, since the ordering of things is nothing other than the manifestation of a spiritual order. In Mies, the new beauty is manifested through subtraction rather than through addition, and in a very strict process that does away with all that is not essential. At that point the two paths separate again. For the minimalists the goal is pure form, the specific object itself. For the architect form never refers to itself, and its essentiality proceeds from what it refers to, a sort of essential and objective principle of volume or of space; that is, of the architectonic.

Judged from these transcendentalist premises, the artist is not the one who creates the form, it is the latter, to the extent in which it is ideal and objective, that is revealed instead. Two years before he died Mies would recall his earlier collaboration with Peter Behrens and affirm that the latter revealed the ur-form, a kind of materialization of essential meaning, to him. "The revelation of the ur-form, which is called on to lend meaning to an era," Mies recalled, "is painstakingly slow to emerge. Not all that occurs occurs on the plane of the visible. The decisive struggles of the spirit take place on invisible battlefields."

If Mies gets this transcendental idea from Behrens, it is from Henrik Berlage that he inherits his interest in

Mies van der Rohe, Farnsworth House, Plano, Illinois, 1946

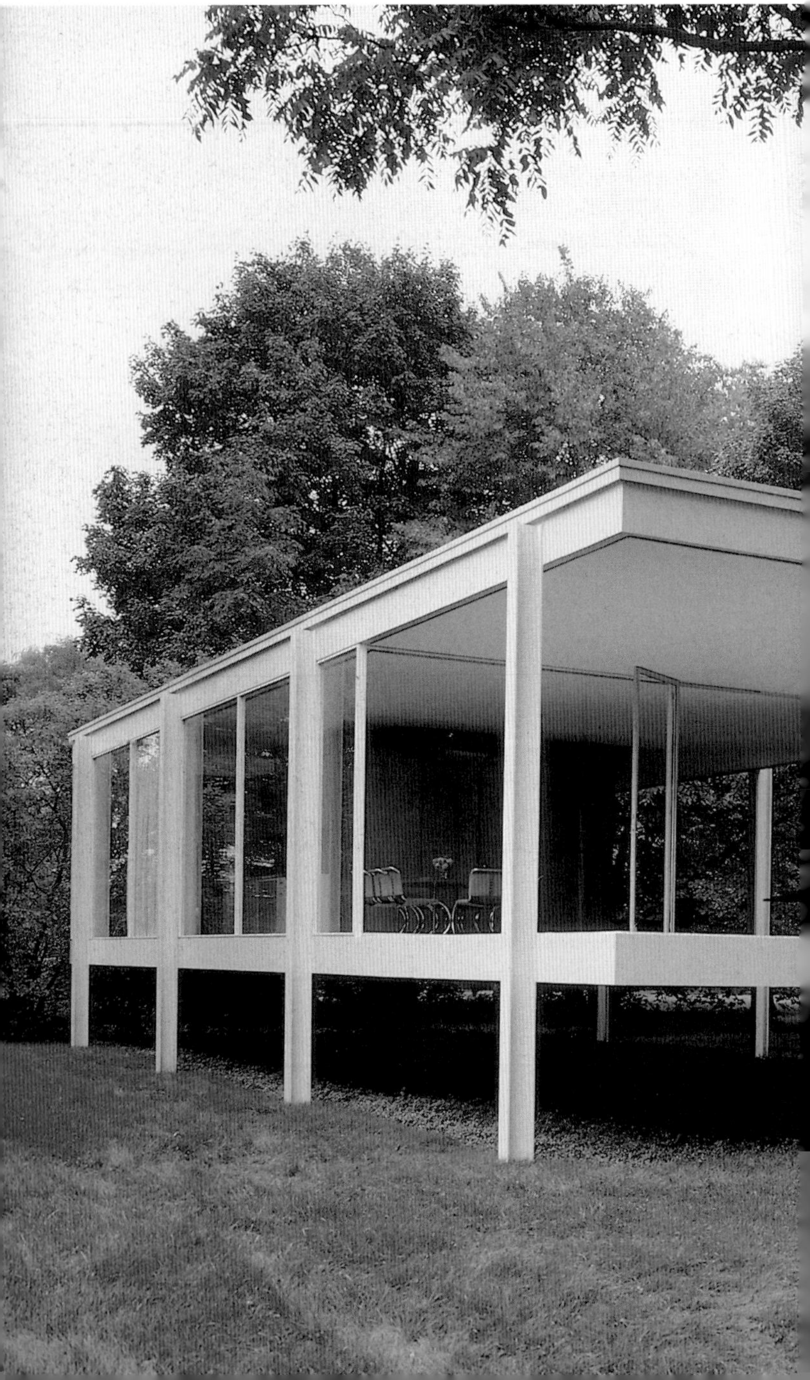

restraint. For the Dutch architect this did not only mean being economical with one's motifs, but included not inventing any. It wasn't a question of inventing forms, but of finding them. "To build is to be useful," Berlage used to say, something which of course separated Mies from Le Corbusier, both of whom would agree that architecture ought to create something, but not what this something is. "To those who say 'architecture must be useful'," Le Corbusier argued, "we reply 'architecture must elicit emotion'." Embarked on the search for emotion, the Purism of the Swiss architect was to be alien to the more radical minimalists.

The idealist radicalism of Mies and the materialist radicalism of sculptural minimalism are what set the two ideas apart, even if these arrive at similar forms. In the relation of sameness that the architect establishes between thought and thing, subject and object, idea and material, the second term is subordinate to the first, which becomes the source of all meaning. Curiously, the success of what, in the widest sense, we might call minimalist language, both sculptural and architectural, has obscured the not wholly viable metaphysical aspects, and focused on the immediately objective: the material element, the object, form.

Nothwithstanding this, transcendentalist theories have generated a discourse discrediting the formal aspect in architecture which, when speaking of the latter as built ideas, persistently subordinates to the invisible the visible, physical and of course technical aspects of the building.

It could be argued that the fear of formalism ends up as a fear of form. Mies himself wasn't able to avoid all the contradictions inherent to this attitude. In 1927, discussing 'On Form in Architecture', he writes: "I am not opposed to form, but only to form as a goal (...) Form as a goal always leads to formalism. It implies, then, an endeavor that is not directed towards the interior, but towards the exterior. But only a living interior can have a living exterior. Any *how* has to be based on a *what*. The non-formalized is no worse than an excess of form. The first is not without significance and the second is appearance." Later he adds:

"We do not privilege the result, but rather the orientation of the process of formalization. It is precisely this that shows us if the form has been encountered as something belonging to life or for itself alone. It's for that reason that the process of formalization is so essential for me."

It is possible that the contradictions in Miesian theory arise from the mixing of purely material terms with moral ones implying subjective judgement. In the case of other languages, starting with human language, structuralism resolved the issue by establishing the arbitrariness of signs, while also recognizing the intimate relationship between signifier and signified. Is there a way of knowing the (profound) *what* other than by recourse to a (superficial) *how*? How does one create a space, if not with constructed, formal elements? In 1931, during a radio broadcast, Mies himself went in that direction: "The artistic structure is added to the objective and functional structure of buildings, or better still, it is consumed in them."

A few years earlier the critic Adolf Behme had addressed the problem: "Rejecting aesthetic speculation, formalism and doctrine is necessary and healthy in itself; it's merely that it seems mistaken to propose this rejection from an anti-aesthetic position, even though we might be perennially against the aesthetics of the aesthetes. Rejecting aesthetic requirements —as opposed to aesthetic speculations— would be tantamount to sawing off the branch we're sitting on."

According to Mies the way of avoiding the kind of formalism associated with historical styles is to have recourse, once again, to an economy of language, meaning that the form no longer derives from the function, but from the structure. By reducing things, then, to what is essential for building, a truly contemporary architecture would be forthcoming whose stylistic contribution lay, as Loos had said, in proposing no style at all and aiming at sobriety and neutral abstraction. For Mies the great edifices are based on structure, this being almost always the bearer of their spatial form, and hence his desire for a streamlined form has its finest ally in the new materials utilized in large buildings. At a certain moment he will even consider the most authentic stage in the construction work as the moment when the metal skeleton of a building has still not been faced with glass.

Abstraction, simple rectilinear geometry, industrial standardization, a precision of finish, literality in the use of materials, austerity and absence of ornament are characteristics common to sculptural minimalism and the ideology of the Modern Movement in architecture. Unconcerned by the prevailing functionalism, Mies van der Rohe put this ideology into practice as no other architect of the century did, even granting it, as we've seen, certain transcendental connotations the artists disdained.

For some, Mies' work itself extends beyond its own contradictions and theoretical transcendentalisms. From this purely formal point of view an architecture that refers to nothing outside itself and makes no appeal to the intellect automatically gives precedence to the direct experience of space and materials. The minimalists would have shared such aims.

Despite everything, what has today become known, under Mies' protective shadow, as minimalist architecture bears the name of some other discipline and method. This would be, up to a point, a sort of revised modernism, a corrected version of a Modern Movement that entered into crisis due to its indiscriminate application as an international style and, as the German architect himself would say, due to having lost a respect for details, for these, according to him and to Flaubert, are where God is. The new architecture would bring modern formal sobriety and the possibilities offered by new materials and new techniques together in a well-versed, knowing sort of modernism.

For many, the challenge continues to be not to move from an expeditious pure functionalism to a pure aestheticism of contemporary abundance, nor to forget the utilitarian character essential to the best architecture because of the dazzling effect produced by extreme gestures. "To applaud Mies," James Marston Fitsch said, "for the monumental purity of his forms and to lament their faulty functioning is like praising the sea for being blue and simultaneously complaining that it's salty, or admiring the tiger for the beauty of its skin and at the same time asking it to become vegetarian."

a minimalist
architecture

Towards reduction

The Industrial Revolution, without which Adolf Loos
or Mies van der Rohe would not have what they were,
brought about a significant change in domestic architecture.
In being displaced to the big cities, the new urban housing
took on unusual forms. Obliged to do so by the increasing
price of land, which was beginning to run out, and thanks
to technical advances, houses started to be heaped one
on top of the other and to grow upwards, helped by new
materials that made their construction both lighter and
cheaper. The dwelling as an architectural entity rapidly
echoed the changes in building technique and was,
furthermore, the setting of the revolution affecting the
everyday life of the individual. Given the sheer abundance
of new commodities, one can say that most dwellings were
doubly transformed.

Until the nineteenth century households in which
the total amount of furniture and goods added up to more
than a hundred objects were rare. Things were thought
of, designed, manufactured and acquired for life, and that
was reason enough for acquiring furniture that was solid
and hard-wearing, over and above any other criterion,
including the aesthetic. After the Industrial Revolution,
homes —which hadn't increased in size, the opposite in
fact— were filled with all kinds of industrial products, useful
and useless, originals and copies, largely aimed at adding
a feeling of luxury that, even as the belongings piled up,
such houses were actually beginning to lose.

Up until that moment furniture, jewelry and decorative
objects were things that obeyed fashions extending over

entire epochs, from one generation to the next. Promoted by industry, the twentieth century multiplied the goods on offer and consequently shortened the time a fashion would last. Before long the new century offered a variety of domestic articles, materials and ideologies that differed according to the decade. In a short space of time the bent wood and wrought iron of *Art Nouveau* found itself existing cheek by jowl with the organic aesthetic of Mollino furniture, the leather and industrial steel of the Bauhaus and Memphis colored plastic of the 70s. This variety and abundance was more often related to accumulation than to replacement. Items of furniture were changed, but for the most part old furniture was retained, rendering movement difficult in houses that unfortunately did not grow at the same speed as the rapidly increasing belongings of their inhabitants.

From the Modern Movement's point of view possessions can be oppressive. This occurs when an object has become obsolete and instead of serving a function, instead of producing pleasure, it only inspires nostalgia. With time, a disused object will interfere with movement, make reaching a shelf difficult, look ugly on top of the television and seem to gather more dust than other objects. One frequently tends to compensate for the reduced size of the home by buying artefacts thought to be luxurious and plentiful. Another potential luxury, that of space, challenges such a capricious accumulation of objects and is, in contrast, associated with order and, up to a point, with control. Spatial luxury is linked to the knowledge of limits, of the moment of stopping, something expressed, for instance, in the Japanese notion of *shibui*, which is nothing other than knowing when to call a halt.

Adaptability to a geographical, material and cultural context, which architects have been striving for ever since Antiquity; technique linked to a region's potential, something that was rehabilitated as a reaction to an excessive modernity; experimenting with local materials; judicious forms of tradition; the applying of criteria decided by climate and customs; the reduction of materials and

73

Tea Pavilion, Katsura Palace, Kyoto

the simplification of forms: these are some of the features
that contrive to elicit the universal criteria of certain local
traditions. We might encounter the foundations of
architectural minimalism in these.

Reduction and synthesis

One of architectural minimalism's main qualities rests
on the idea of reduction: faced with excess and disorder,
to reduce in order to purify, so as to be able to choose,
to know how to proceed. John Pawson, the English
architect who has made minimalism his hallmark, defines
this procedure, applied to art, architecture and design,
as the quality a building has when each component, each
detail, each join and each bearing has been reduced or
condensed to its essence. The difference between a good
architect and a bad one, Ludwig Wittgenstein said, is that
the bad architect falls into each and every temptation, while
the good one resists them. "Avoiding the irrelevant,"
Pawson has said, "is the way to emphasize the important."
The road towards the minimum embraces reduction and,
as such, presupposes a choice, a search for the essence
of a space whose components would be schematically
limited without being diminished, circumscribed to the
point of nothingness. Minimalism, then, might seem to
be the style of no-style, and nothing is further from reality.
Or from its novelty.

A quick reading of the chronological map of the history
of art reveals cycles of reductive cultures extending over
a wide spectrum, from the primitive —due to torpor,
immediacy or lack of means— to modernism, and this
because of an idea and a revolution in attitude. At times first
impressions, the deformed or the schematic are the things
that can best explain the forms. Classical cultures practised
a selecting of contents, aimed at purifying the forms, which
naturally also limited its options. From this point of view,
minimalism as a style would remain one mid-possibility
of origins as equanimously classical as they are essential,
or primitive, falsely so.

In reduction, and in any selective process, the problem
that instantly arises is the need to define the essential. As to

John Pawson, RK RK clothes shop, London, 1991

that definition we are obviously on subjective ground. Is a chair essential? Not for some African cultures or for traditional Japanese culture. Things being so, one cannot argue about the essentiality of certain components or details of the chair back, or the chair seat, without instantly questioning the basic necessity of said object. Reduction could be, perhaps, a general term that might be applied to any one of the household effects used in differing traditions and cultures. Are we talking about absolute reduction —of functions and uses— as a reaction to social, cultural and environmental issues, or are we merely talking about a reduction of forms?

In the Middle Ages the Cistercian Order, wanting architecture to help define a simpler form of Christianity, had its monasteries built according to precise instructions on how to use undressed stone and put up walls without color or ornamentation. Decoration, the monks argued, was distracting the devout attention of their followers. A plainness of finish lent monumentality to such buildings, and their effect increased by being reduced to a single impression instead of dispersed focuses of attention. The reductive essentiality of minimalism would unite those ancient cultures with more recent ones resulting from the sophistication of industry. It would also unite the wealthier classes with the more modest, and at times more farflung, ones. Japan and various Berber peoples, for example, would speak the same language. From that viewpoint, minimalism would become universal, if we accept its reductive, and at the same time exalting, application in each different cultural situation.

Alfred Hitchcock used to say that in cinema what doesn't add up subtracts. For his part Gaudí claimed that if he was constructing such complicated plans it was because he didn't know enough to make them simple, and the writer Antoine de Saint-Exupéry stated that when trying to improve a work one should not ask oneself what could be added to it, but what could be taken away. A rule of thumb with which Mies van der Rohe would agree, Mies being the man who welcomed, and popularized, the phrase "less is more" coined by his teacher Peter Behrens. In the

Le Thoronet Abbey, Thoronet, France, 1190

'most least' defended by the German architect, the 'most' was, curiously, the 'least': the details. Just as with Mies van der Rohe, like-minded minimalists such as the Japanese designer Shiro Kuramata or the Mexican architect Luis Barragán treated design as something which, more than adding things, involved learning to choose; that is, involved starting to omit them.

Reduction, the search for the essential, relies on selection, then, and in that sifting process, the details that would characterize minimal spaces are invisible details registered because they are lacking or only found when looked for. And so, at a remove from visual obstacles and ostentatious ornamentations, in minimalist spaces one admires a bearing for the naturalness of its union, and a socle for the floating effect its absence produces in the wall. Minimalist space is the locus of the subtle, so much so that to its critics it manages to appear as the realm of the void.

Taken to its maximum degree, reduction is an indispensable condition of architectural minimalism. The idea, as we saw, is not new. Simplicity has been sought after by the ideals of many cultures. Architectural minimalism partakes of that same search from such seemingly disparate viewpoints and motivations as the freedom pursued by Thoreau, resulting from contact with the essential side of existence, or the Zen conception of beauty as truth and extreme bareness.

A moral dimension to plainness

To lack belongings is to possess the world. This is the voluntary poverty defended by Zen thinking. In the words of Buddha: "A man weighed down by his belongings is like a vessel that ships water. The only hope of reaching dry land consists in throwing the cargo overboard." We must not forget that man, in essence, originally possesses nothing, Buddha, a man who revealed himself, in his own comportment, to be against an excess that instead of enriching life impoverishes it, reminds us.

The Japanese concept, *wabi*, the quality that comes from voluntary poverty, is both a moral principle and

Zen Garden, Ryoanji Temple, Kyoto

an aesthetic rule. Just as in the Buddhist teachings, it warns against an impoverishing excess. *Wabi* refers to the beauty of incomplete, variable and non-conventional things, an idealist beauty that restores good sense, measure and an extreme anti-rationalism to the idea of creation. *Wabi-sabi* means simple, without artifice, incomplete, non-sophisticated, the basis needed for being able to appreciate the tiniest details of everyday life. From within this silent, undistracted framework it is possible to appreciate the unsuspected aspects of nature, of place. *Wabi-sabi* is also about the delicate balance between the pleasure things give us and the pleasure we attain in freeing ourselves of them. This is an idea that's easy to imagine yet difficult to conceptualize, however.

Many religions share an ideal of poverty that culminates in non-ownership. From Zen Buddhism to the domestic and social organization of the Protestant Quakers, material poverty linked to spiritual richness has been insistently preached by the most diverse creeds. Reduced to the essential, to the minimum, minimalism pleads for a certain truth, an authenticity of place and object, a bareness that is far cry from expressionism, yet which attains expressivity. A radicalism for which, according to Le Corbusier and Mies, a special disposition of the spirit is needed. One might detect a certain animosity towards that search for geometrical purity, for a spatial sense of calm and repose. The process of reduction, of synthesis, via which spaces dispense with their facings and partitions in order to be open to the light and devoid of furniture, could be read as an act of purification of a place. Nevertheless, the minimalist style is certainly not an abject or economical one, sensually speaking.

An architecture that uses repetition, balance, order, plus a reduced set of geometric figures, materials and colors, reaches out to that simplicity so difficult to attain and so long sought after. We have to distinguish, however, between the most practical and the most simple. An undeniable feature of minimalist architecture is its precision of execution, something that is, to be sure, very costly, and not just in economic terms.

A minimalist architecture?

Unlike the Modern Movement, today's architectonic minimalism does not reject decoration, but avoids it by absorbing it. Instead of opting for universal solutions, it makes a universal idea out of individual resources. It doesn't link truth to structure, as did Mies van der Rohe, but tends towards a constitutional bareness, even privileging the essentiality of the non-structural elements.

Any account of minimalist buildings would embrace compact edifices with simple, rectilinear geometries, plus uniform, uninterrupted facades that, because of their plainness and severity, also have their echo in the history of architecture. The quasi-monolithic simplicity of some of these interventions seeks to concentrate expression, contain it in a single eloquent gesture. Concentration, reduction and selection go to form the basic features of a possible minimalist architecture. Such a way of doing things would be typified, urbanistically, by adroit gestures and essential geometries resulting from the work of synthesis.

The flat shapes and simple volumes become functional for the building when they are respectful towards the city, and contribute, through their restraint, to organizing the often chaotic urban space. Being uniform, monochrome, unbroken and devoid of ornament, the facades of such buildings present a striking, often monumental vision, plus, paradoxically, a false image of the building's weight. The visual density of this movement would, then, be one more perceptual effect of the reducing of its language and of the uniformity and impact of its facades, not always as the outcome of using heavyweight materials. In a return to the simplest, most Cartesian order, in which the options are limited and the basic norm consists in reducing things, mistakes may occur, almost exclusively, from the breaching of those few norms.

We find, then, among minimalist buildings simple and striking geometrical volumes and subtly sophisticated finishes. The facades, which for the modernists were a barrier between the interior and exterior space of the building, take

Kazuyo Sejima, Saishunkan Women's Dormitory, Kumamoto, Japan, 1991

Herzog & de Meuron, Goetz Collection, Munich, 1992

on a starring role in minimalism. Hence, certain flat and monochrome architectonic skins can become screens, filters of their mass.

Wrapped in the translucent glass surfaces of its facade, the structure of the Goetz Collection Gallery that Herzog & de Meuron created in Munich (1992) profits from the effect of opacity. The Swiss architects have also turned to this solution in their rehabilitation of the London headquarters of the Tate Gallery. Apart from being a thermal and acoustic insulator, its double glass is a kind of veil which announces, without revealing, the reverse side of a facade.

The uniform, evocative, dense and very smooth new skins again assume an anti-modernist quality: they cover the architectural masses or conceal these by adapting them to their context, helping contain and reduce the building itself. Facades are converted into continuous planes of the one material: concrete, stone, or a curtain wall in huge sections. Using opaque or translucent materials, they reduce the connection between interior and exterior and also undermine the relationship between matter and structure, two things the modernist credo emphasized. In minimalism a reduced, and at the same time extended, version of modernism is at work, though. This would include a rigorously applied, and thus intensified, lack of ornament; the use of simple geometric volumes, reduced to rectilinear forms; angles, preferably right-angles, and the supposed universality of their language, a language which can, although this doesn't always happen, allow for a modulation of the different accents of local materials. Thus, certain of Peter Zumthor's works, like Les Bains in Vals (1996) or the Kunsthaus in Bregenz (1997), shed their skin, and wood substitutes for stone or glass according to the local tradition, the possibilities, the needs or the context in which the buildings are constructed.

For the French writer André Gide glass was the greatest enemy of mystery and awareness. For his part, Einstein spoke of mystery as the most beautiful experience there was, and one of the foremost historians of modern architecture, Siegfried Giedion, considered the visitor, passer-by or observer to be an active participant in the

Peter Zumthor, Thermal Baths, Vals, Switzerland, 1996

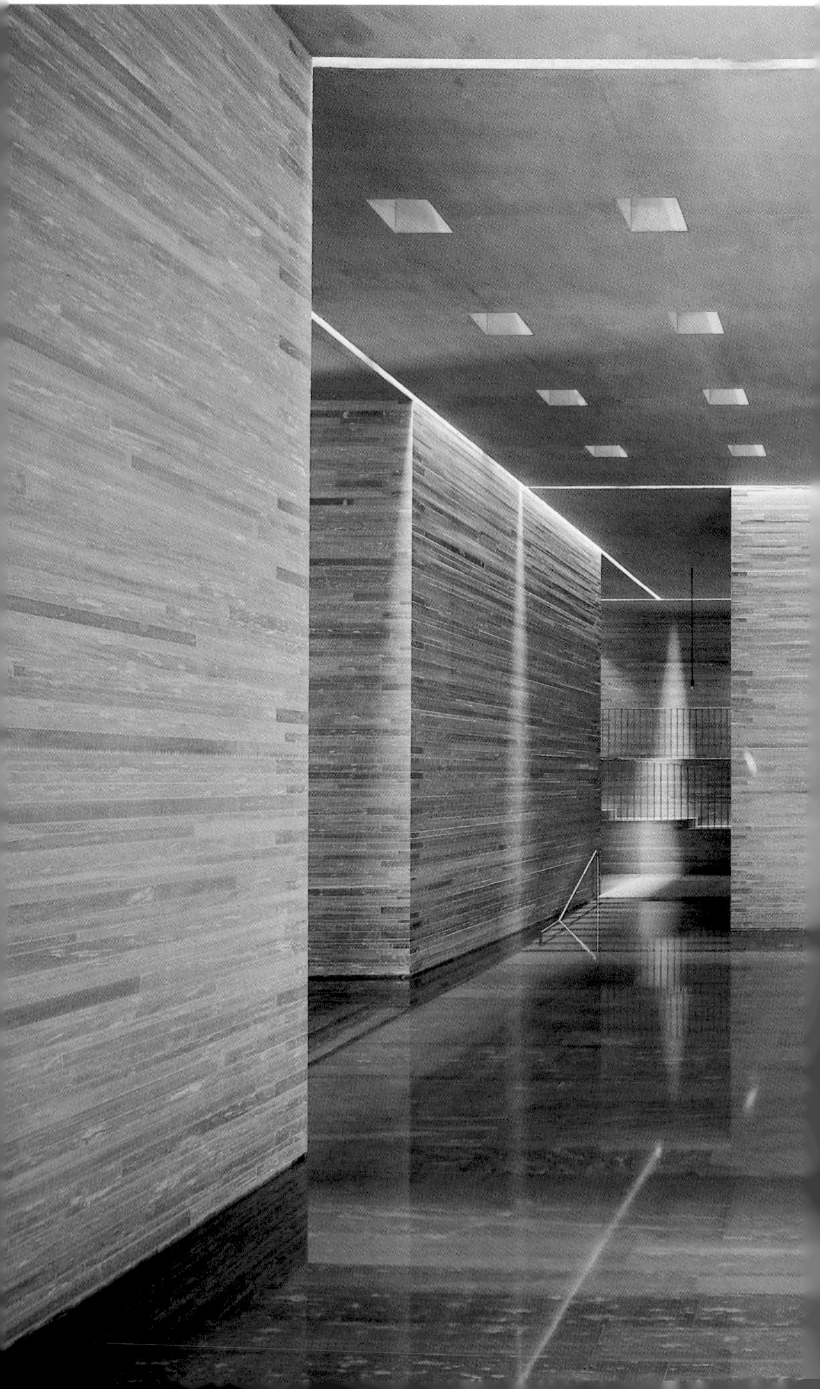

32°

shaping of buildings and spaces. The more ambiguous and indeterminate these spaces are, the more the interested spectator will participate in them. An apparent dematerialization will therefore signpost the road towards a minimalist architecture.

Dematerialization

To the absence of separate elements, the lack of typological references and the clean lines of minimalist facades, one would, in the costly and painstaking job of rendering the construction invisible, have to add other internal omissions motivated by the search for purity and the reducing of the components defining a space. Hence, to a progressive reduction that extends, for example, to the lack of plinths, one could equally add the use of discreet, hidden and even invisible constructional features: the integration of lighting and built-in shelving, the reducing of door- and window-frames to a few millimeters, the transparency of partition walls, the absence of knobs and handles, the substitution of protuberances by fissures, and a whole range of careful finishes that call for tremendous precision in their manufacture and placement.

When constructing minimalist spaces the vast size of the elements used is all-important. In parquet flooring, stone paving or facade curtain walls, the scale of the modules used is huge in order not to break up the physical and visual regularity of the volumes. One arrives, due to that unbroken aspect, at a uniform and ordered reading of the surfaces. The disappearance of the joins, of the combination and alternation of materials highlights the disappearance of the material itself. Just as the trees in a leafy wood, when seen from afar, seem to disappear, in the facades of minimalist buildings the materials become imperceptible.

The visual dematerialization of minimalist architecture may be an echo of other sociological reactions prompted, once again, by the development of industry and advances in technology. Just as certain once-physical media like music and film become immaterial by being computerized, so the typological identification of certain architectures disappears in minimalist architecture. In this instance the combination of limited resources and scarcity of materials has, however, a fundamentally aesthetic and oddly functional rationale. From this mixture there result polyvalent spaces that are easier to maintain. The minimalist style —which can be a style with intentional gaps and empty spaces, but never a lack of style— might function, furthermore, in opposition to the supposed precariousness and obsolescence habitual in commercial interiors. Just as the most classical kinds of clothes turn out to be, in reality, the least defined in fabric, form and color, so the most neutral architecture could also be the most resilient.

Veering towards dematerialization, the Japanese designer Shiro Kuramata showed in the mid-80s that one could maintain the spirit of poverty contained in the notion of *wabi,* and so devote oneself to propagating the minimalist style without neglecting advances in technology and the potential of new materials. The easy chair *How High Is the Moon* (1985) reproduced the traditional form of a high-back chair while reducing its visible weight, mass and surface to a mere wisp of metal. The Issey Miyake boutique in Shibuya, Tokyo (1987) would result, shortly afterwards, from the designer applying his ideas of lightness and dematerialization to space.

It is no mere chance that another restless spirit on the world architecture scene, Philip Johnson, would construct what he called his Ghost House (1985) in the garden of his residence in New Canaan, Connecticut. Almost 90, Johnson, the designer who would coin, spread and adopt almost all the architectural tendencies the century has seen, erected a small dwelling of metal mesh. More sculptural than architectonic, and as economical as it is unlivable in, his undertaking involved the simplest way of carving out a private space. The poverty, humility and lightness of the materials used betold an individual, open construction —of technical expertise and economic demands— stemming from both an ultra-modernism and an archaic primitivism.

Alongside this, other architects like Toyo Ito have manifested a shared interest in the visual qualities of

Shiro Kuramata, *How High Is the Moon* armchair, 1987

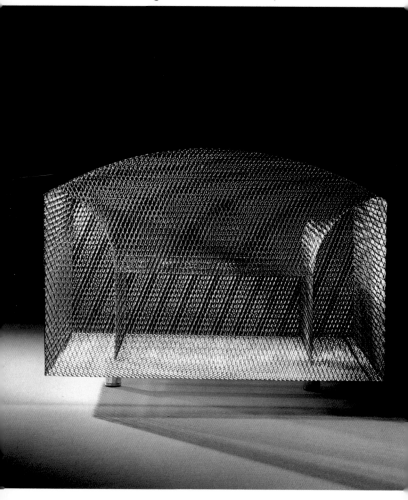

Philip Johnson, Ghost House, New Canaan, USA, 1985

imperceptible materials and, influenced by certain aspects of contemporary culture and technology, in the electronic media and designing by computer as well. Projects like Tower of the Winds, which Ito would erect in Yokohama in 1986, and which is strongly reminiscent of the glass skyscraper Mies designed in 1922 for Berlin, or like the leisure-time study by Kaako, Laine, Liimatainen and Tirkkonen in Espoo (Finland) in 1992, or like Bernard Tschumi's Videogallery in Groningen in 1991, reflect on architecture as a linguistic corpus by debating the relationship between architecture and meaning, and also between visual perception and structure.

In 1990-91 the Americans Tod Williams and Billie Tsien were invited by the choreographer Elisa Monte to create the sets for a dance performance, *The World Upside-Down*. The architects also used translucent materials, in this instance an extremely fine mesh fabric, to construct a movable backdrop. Behind the lit-up background there moved the shadows of the performers who were participating in the show. The scenographic components would disappear in this intervention, and with them, the performers —who were reduced to two-dimensional shadows— in an attempt to dematerialize the effect of this being theater.

The dematerialization of architecture is, in essence, as paradoxical as it is impossible, yet the immaterial tendency which affects, in a fragmentary and gradual way, the various elements and devices making up a building is an incontrovertible fact. And so, to the absence of plinths, handrails and lamps, one would have to add the lack of logoes, which in some businesses have been substituted by graphic projections, simpler and cheaper to change, yet more eye-catching to present. The projection of the names and logoes of bars and shops and the sight of set designs derived from varying projections points to the immanent projection of decoration in which color and two-dimensional stylistic devices could be altered in a matter of seconds. Projections on the facades of different buildings reinforce the notional idea of changeable, two-dimensional facings and decorations, alternatable and, of course, intangible.

**Kaakko, Laine, Liimatainen, Tirkkonen, Leisure Workshop,
Espoo, Finland, 1992**

Mies van der Rohe, Glass Skyscraper, model, Berlin, 1922

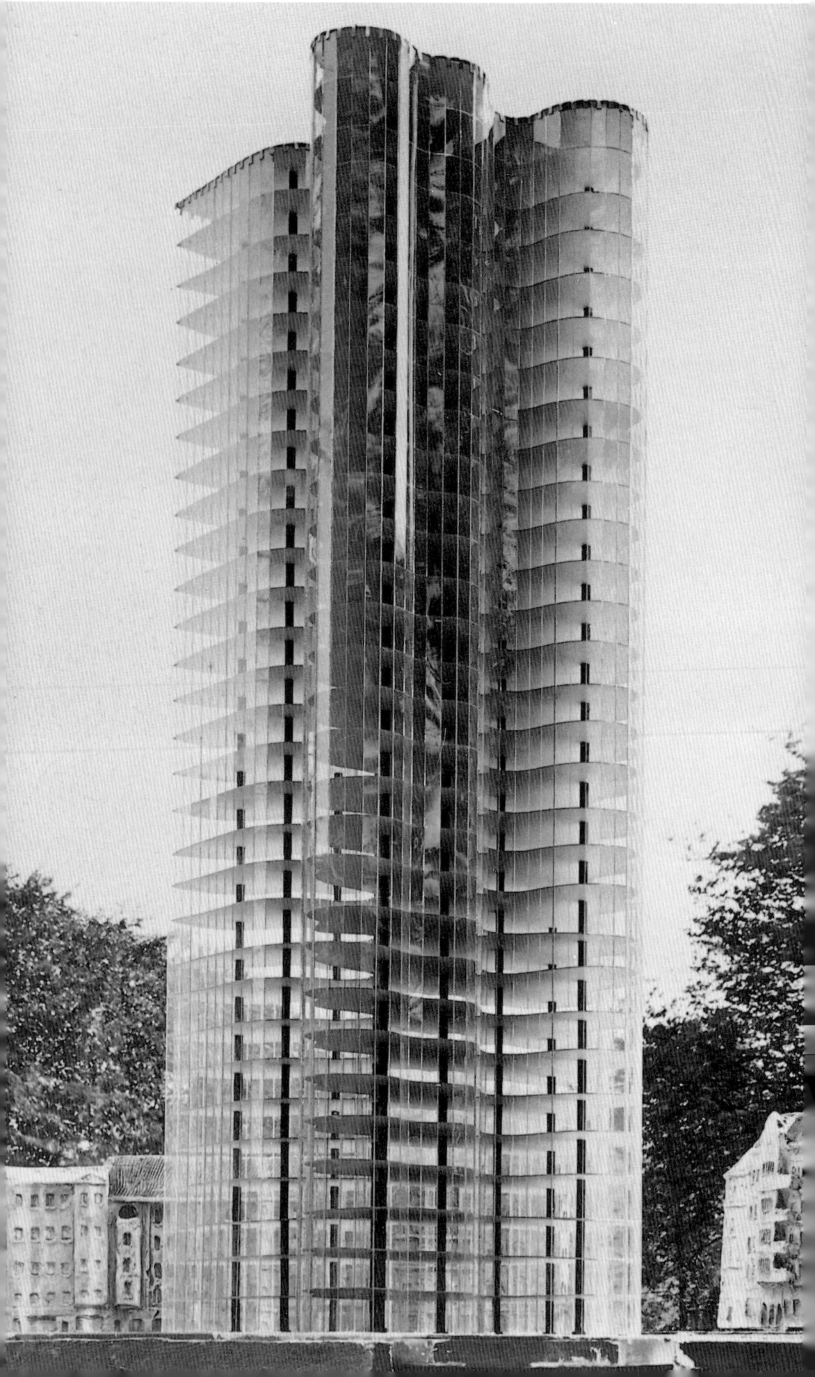

Toyo Ito, Tower of the Winds, Yokohama, Japan, 1986-1995

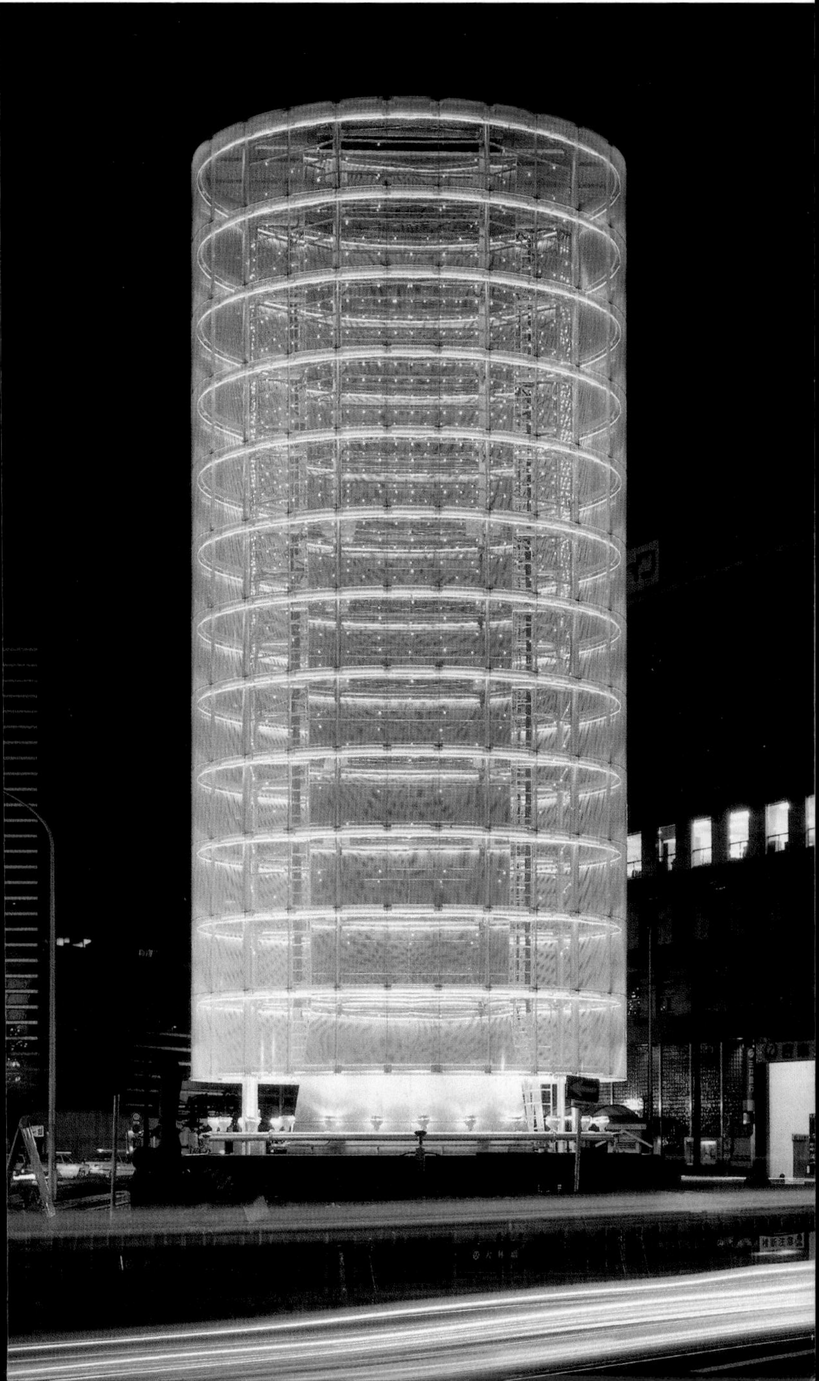

Bernard Tschumi, Glass Video Gallery, Groningen, Holland, 1990

Williams Tsien, *The World Upside-Down*, stage design, Amsterdam, New York, 1990-1991

A fresh mystery

The British architect John Pawson, who openly and radically champions the virtues of minimalism in his works, counsels against the use of panes of glass and of the effects of transparency. "Within the minimalist context," he argues, "a transparent wall might be too visible." It has to be remembered that in architectural minimalism omission seeks to be suggestion, and that our attention is claimed by absence and nothingness, though never by excess or transparency. In minimalism glass functions as a veil, as insinuation. The Cannelle patisserie (1988) that Pawson himself built in London proposes a wise and witty use of mystery by cutting out, in the middle of a large screen-printed glass pane, a transparent square in which a single cake is exhibited. For their part, Herzog & de Meuron have sometimes given their buildings a floating quality. They've obtained striking lighting effects thanks to glass, plus revealing or suggestive facades due to working with known but new technical methods: glass treated by sand-blasting, with acid or covered in algae.

The facade of the Kirchner Museum in Davos (1992), by the Swiss architects Gigon & Guyer, was built with a glass which does not let one see anything apart from the glass itself; a glass similar to that used by Claus en Kaan in his Amsterdam house (1995) or by Peter Zumthor for the Art Museum in Bregenz. In both instances this means a translucent prism made of concrete and glass, of museums that emphasize one of the features of architectural minimalism which, unlike the Modern Movement, deliberately separates, as we saw, the skin from the structure of the building, its truth from its support. Thus, and although the exterior is faced in glass, in Zumthor's Austrian museum the galleries are perimetrally enclosed by concrete walls and receive overhead light alone, thus avoiding harmful direct light.

Minimalism, then, appears to want to reduce everything, apart from the mystery of architecture. Just as the progressive dematerialization can be pointed to of certain functions without these disappearing altogether —concealed lighting, an absence of plinths and walls

John Pawson, Cannelle cake shop, London, 1988

Claus en Kaan, Haarlemmerbuurt Housing, Amsterdam, 1995

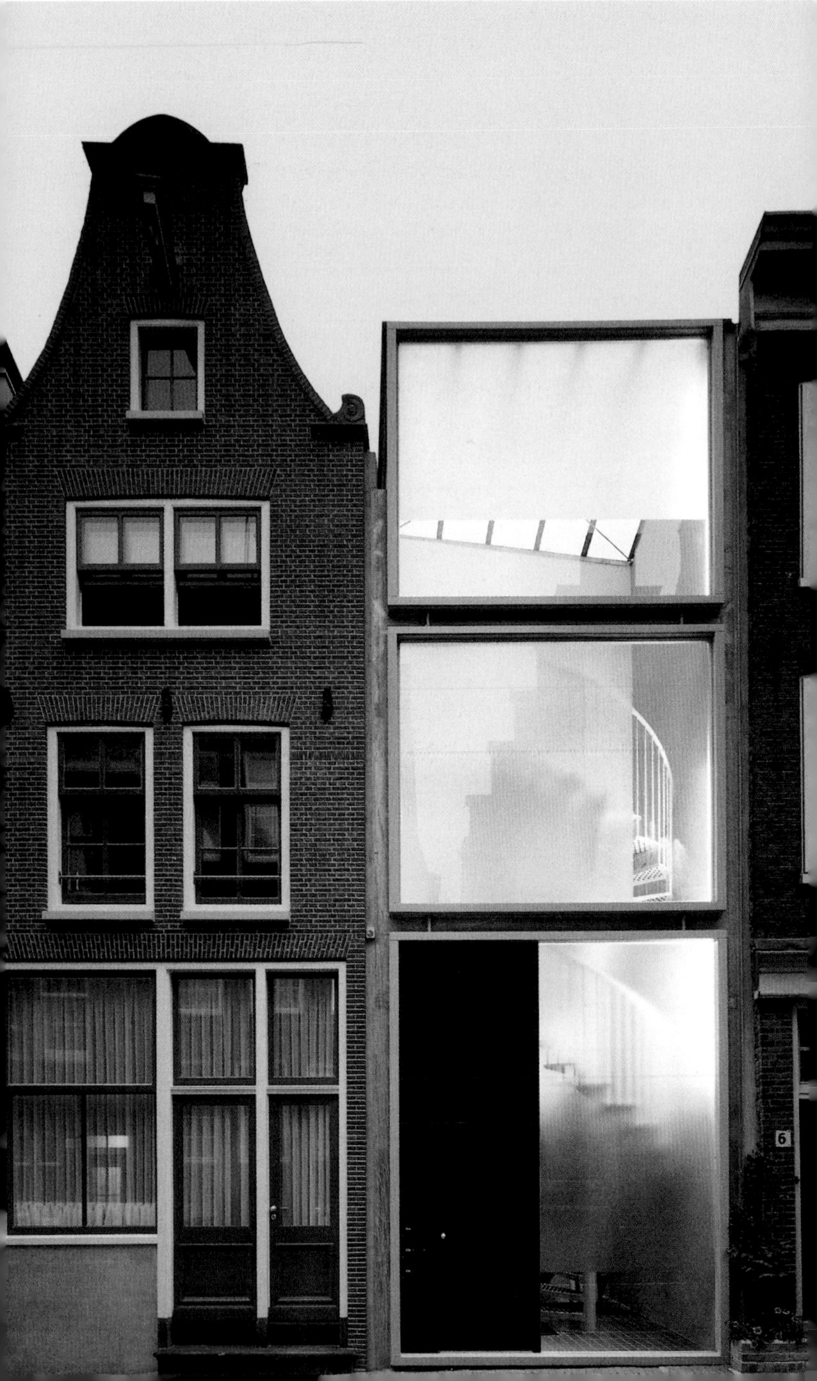

erected to avoid friction—, so the cold sensuality of Herzog & de Meuron's buildings, for instance, has been alluded to. For the Swiss architects their attention to materials and to the uniformity of planes now appears as a *'dénomination d'origine'*, a guarantee that is subject to the setting and function of the building. Geometrical rigor and a quasi-intellectual approach to materials are combined in their classically ornamented facades, understanding classicism in its non-historical sense, without quotations.

Unlike the cold calculations of the Modern Movement, minimalism makes every effort to avoid coldness, to be subtle and plain, yet approachable. It is, paradoxically, a contemporary attitude that is frequently more artisanal than industrial, and for that reason the interplay of living materials such as wood means that its interiors are not overly pure or aseptic. Natural fibers, pale-colored stone, different types of wood and whitewash point up, with their subtle and neutral colors, the limpid minimalist interior.

There exists, among the architects associated with this style, a sensual or intellectual approach to materials. Over and above functional usage or budgetary limitations, for some of these designers their materials obey the forms and the work expended for their creation. Thus Zumthor defines a relationship with matter that is both Beckettian and Proustian, punchy and nostalgic, a relationship in which the physical referents encounter links with their own infancy or with sensations evoked by the materials themselves. "The forms," he says, "that everyday life has ordained over time, the forms daily usage has charged with significance. The sound of footsteps, interior load-bearing facades and exterior ones that allude drastically and also moderately to their context." The tectonic distances itself from the construction in order to take root in its own image of construction. As Mies would say, the construction goes back to being construction.

Minimalism appeals to the subtle, to the evanescent, to what is visible beyond the ordinary gaze, and yet from plainness it attains monumentality. Many of these buildings are striking in their discretion, are monumental without being spectacular. The monumentality of minimalist

Peter Zumthor, Kunsthaus, Bregenz, Austria, 1998

architecture is seemingly deferential because restrained, and therefore strange. The buildings belonging to this movement are discreet, and thus they contribute more to consolidating the urban fabric than to breaking it up. The other side of the coin of that monumental gesture is the buildings' maintainance. Just as in a face without eyebrows, in an edifice without window frames, cornices, canopies or friezes, expression might seem a minus, and protection, the maintenance of the building, a plus. It would be paradoxical if a neutral and restrained building, designed, notwithstanding fashions and clever gestures, for a long life, couldn't endure, was defeated by the coming and going of fashions rather than by the erosion of time. A number of maintenance solutions have been repeatedly used by those architects who have closed ranks around minimalism. Devices such as inclined ramps, so as not to break up the planes, walls that do not touch the ground, protective juts or the use of fine materials that aid maintenance, then, extend the life and guarantee the pure look of many of these buildings. Precision of execution, which slows down the construction of these plain-looking buildings and makes them expensive, is their main weapon against deterioration and the passing of time.

A specific typology

With the elimination of window frames, partition walls and doorways, unadorned, uninterrupted space becomes the real protagonist of this type of planning. Obviated or assimilated decoration, incorporated or reduced detail leads to the construction of volumes and spaces in which a value is attached to the architecture through space itself, through the pure and exclusively architectonic features of this. Given the painstaking attention to all its elements, the all-over look it acquires and, above all, the radical importance interior design has in minimalist architecture, the latter would link up with older forms of integrated architecture in which the architect was meticulously designing every single detail of a scheme: from the structure itself down to the ashtrays, and including the doorknobs, bathroom fittings, furniture and landscaping. It is this notion of overall evaluation that, over and above a particular style, might prompt one to speak of a minimalist ambience.

The writer Paul Scheerbat claimed that the acolytes of the Bauhaus had invented spaces on which it was hard to leave a fingerprint, something Bertolt Brecht and Walter Benjamin saw as an advantage. "Rub out all traces," Brecht says to the city-dweller. For his part, Benjamin wrote on the poverty of experience. "It isn't necessary to believe that men yearn for new experience. No, they yearn to free themselves of experiences, they yearn for a world around which they can make their poverty, external and finally internal too, take on such simple and evident validity that something decorous grows out of it. They aren't always ignorant or inexpert. It's often possible to claim the opposite: they have 'devoured' everything, 'culture' and 'man', and they're surfeited and exhausted."

The *tabula rasa* that the essentialism of certain architects postulates takes to the extreme the modernist idea of constructing altered exteriors that are interchangeable and typologically neutral, thus lending a compact, ambiguous and at times mysterious appearance to their buildings. Minimalism shows itself to be in thrall to the interior, to a paradoxical, or consistently vacant, interior. It is not surprising, then, that it is in interior design itself that minimalist architecture encounters its specific typology. A rigorous space, visible in the detail and invisible in terms of impact, might form the perfect frame for an exhibition space. Museums, galleries, exhibition and commercial centers are typologies in which the denuded architecture mustn't enter into competition with the product on show, meaning that it is the product itself which typologically differentiates the space or serves as commercial publicity.

With the glazing of the facade, commercial premises are instantly converted into shop window displays, which means that during the day natural light is made good use of, and that by night the whole building is transformed into its own lit-up advertising announcement. Naturally, this discreet super-exposure causes problems of maintenance, such as a greater sensitivity to climactic changes or a seeming vulnerability to theft, which the architect will have to solve with foresight and the appropriate features and materials.

In minimalist commercial premises, thought of as light-boxes, advertising logoes become bits of writing that are subtly introduced into, printed on, or subtracted from the actual facade of the building. The Lisson Gallery Tony Fretton would build in London (1991) converts a flat facade into something of a puzzle for the interested spectator. In the Johan (1994) the Claudio Silvestrin boutique in Graz the lighting and merchandise display as a whole is built into the architecture of the premises. In the shop he would plan for Calvin Klein in Tokyo (1994), Pawson cut out the designer's name in one of the premises' walls. It's no longer the name, brand or image, then, that distinguishes the business but the new ambience the space projects. The reticent architecture of minimalism itself is rendered visible through the invisibility of its component parts. In such empty spaces, let's remember, order and discipline are *de rigueur*. In the Natan fashion store Vincent van Duysen would build in Amberes (1994) the clothes are displayed inside and on top of monolithic blocks that can be read as minimalist sculptures. Thus, the selection process at the moment of displaying the merchandise will have to be rigorous. A highly limited display of objects is a double-edged sword: it intimidates the passer-by by declaring the exclusivity of what is displayed, and it encourages him to enter the premises to check out the other goods on offer. On top of that, arrangement and grouping helps in the internal observation of the premises by offering an unobstructed view from any one point of this.

Obviously, selective displaying of the merchandise is only possible in an uncluttered setting. The cleaning-up of interior space requires, furthermore, concealing the installations, sophistication in the bearings, ingenuity in the fixtures and complete precision in the joining of the various materials. To be sure, these aspects bring us to the major paradox of this style: its high cost, dictated by the handcrafted details, the one-off nature of the solutions employed and the quality of the materials. In the Rui Alberto art galleries in Lisbon (1991), Eduardo Souto

Tony Fretton, Lisson Gallery, London, 1991

Claudio Silvestrin, Johan shop, Graz, 1994

John Pawson, Calvin Klein store, New York, 1995

Eduardo Souto de Moura, Frame shop Rui Alberto I, Porto, 1991

**Eduardo Souto de Moura, Frame shop Rui Alberto 3,
Vila Nova de Gaia, 1996**